NORTHAMPTON
WELCOME TO THE PAST
—— *PART THREE* ——
Out and About

Frontispiece. Richard Hearne, better known as Mr Pastry, hitches a ride on a 1902 vintage Wolsley while making a collection for worthy causes on Sunday 16 October 1960. The ensemble forms part of Chipperfield's Circus Parade as they swing into Derngate from St Giles Square, en route from Castle station to Midsummer Meadow where the circus would be performing during the week.

(Northampton Chronicle & Echo)

NORTHAMPTON
WELCOME TO THE PAST

PART THREE

Out and About

by

RICHARD COLEMAN and JOE RAJCZONEK

W.D. WHARTON
Wellingborough

First published in 1997

W.D. Wharton
37 Sheep Street
Wellingborough
Northamptonshire NN8 1BX

Text copyright © Richard Coleman and Joe Rajczonek 1997

Richard Coleman and Joe Rajczonek assert their moral right
to be identified as the authors of this work

ISBN 0 9518557 9 4

Designed by John Hardaker, Wollaston, Northamptonshire
Printed and bound in Great Britain by
Butler & Tanner Ltd
Frome, Somerset

ACKNOWLEDGEMENTS

We would like to express our thanks to all those who have helped us with photographs and information during the compiling of this book, especially the photographers from the *Northampton Chronicle & Echo*, whose work, with the kind permission of the Editor, once again forms the backbone of these volumes.

In particular, we thank John Meredith for allowing us to use his father's photographs; and Angie Hogan for the use of her father's (A. J. Bennett) photographic collection; Chris Clayson for the loan of photographs; Les Hanson for photographs and information; Ted Lloyd and Robert Wharton for the loan of items from their respective photographic collections; John Morrison and Ron Thompson, of Northampton Borough Council, for the tram painting on the back jacket and Neil Coates, of the *Northampton Chronicle & Echo*, for his invaluable assistance.

For help with information we also thank Marion Arnold and Colin Eaton of the Northamptonshire Reference Libraries; Brian Hornsey and Don Hickling for information about the town's cinemas; the Town Hall staff; Judith Hodgkinson and, for help with information on canals, David Blagrove; Richard Moisey, Trevor Stainwright and Jeff Stainwright for their assistance.

Our thanks, too, go to Tom Rajczonek for photographic printing; to John Hardaker for putting the book together, retouching the digitized photographic images and dealing with our amendments; and last but not least to Robert Wharton who, as publisher, continues to support our efforts to record in words and pictures our local heritage.

~

Half title caption
A dramatic sky over Abington Square on Tuesday 19 July 1960 silhouettes the Edgar Mobbs memorial statue to artistic effect. *(Northampton Chronicle & Echo)*

Title page caption
25 feet high and 10 feet wide, these stunning Christmas chandeliers were enough to gladden the heart as they lit up Gold Street on the otherwise miserable wet Saturday night of 19 November 1960. *(Northampton Chronicle & Echo)*

Front end-paper captions
(Left) A novel demonstration of joint advertising at Abington Square on Tuesday 15 December 1959 with a novel vehicle in the shape of a Heinkel bubble car. *(Northampton Chronicle & Echo)*

(Right) Friday 10 January 1964 was one of those wet, cold and overcrowded days in Fish Street, long before any thoughts of pedestrianisation. *(Northampton Chronicle & Echo)*

Rear end-paper captions
(Left) Street urchins keep their eye on the photographer as he takes a picture of Arundel Street from Priory Street on Wednesday 10 May 1967, which is not surprising really considering that 209 properties in the area were about to be compulsorily purchased for demolition. *(Northampton Chronicle & Echo)*

(Right) Jim Wagstaff sets out from Northampton to walk to Singapore on Friday 1 May 1959. *(Northampton Chronicle & Echo)*

CONTENTS

INTRODUCTION

SINCE the publication of the first two volumes of *Northampton – Welcome to the Past* we have been inundated with requests for further volumes, and in response we have once more worked our magic to put together a collection of top quality photographs showing yet more of the events – serious and light-hearted – that have taken place in Northampton over the years, as well as views of the fine old buildings and other features which became victims of development and are now a fast fading memory in the minds of those who have lived their lives in the town. In doing this we have been helped greatly by the *Northampton Chronicle & Echo*, but there are also pictures from other sources.

The book's 200 plus photographs include scenes of royal and celebrity visits, special events and parades. Here, too, you can see the Cobblers football team in its glory days, and another fascinating and nostalgic collection of street scenes, including a series of overhead shots taken from high rooftops and from the air in the 1960s.

Also portrayed is shopping in the town as it once was in the days of local family businesses before the supermarket era swept most of them away. There is a section devoted to the emergency services at work around the town in the 1960s, and another on local waterways.

Indeed, there is something for everyone in this new selection of photographs carefully chosen for quality and nostalgic impact, all of which complement those in our first two books on the town, and the three volumes together form a unique, valuable and memory-jogging pictorial record of 'the good old days' in Northampton.

Time and time again we are contacted by people who recognise friends and relatives in the pictures in our books, and by those who are moved to relate their own memories of a particular event or part of town. Many also show us photographs that they took themselves at the time, and we are always delighted to see them, especially when these are of sufficient quality and interest for inclusion in our books.

Richard Coleman and Joe Rajczonek

ON PARADE

1. Chipperfield's Circus arrives in town once again on Sunday 16 October 1960, making its way along Marefair, headed by the band of No. 5 Squadron Air Training Corps, progressing towards Midsummer Meadow from Castle Station. All the buildings behind them have long since been demolished, with Grose's garage and F. F. Tee, the well-known baker, relocating to other parts of the town. *(Northampton Chronicle & Echo)*

2. Children and adults look on in admiration as a pair of elephants and their handlers take a stroll from Marefair into Gold Street on Thursday 5 November 1959 while advertising Roberts Brothers' Circus which was appearing in the town. The following day the two elephants, named Baby and Rebecca, toured the town collecting money for 'World Refugee Year', with Rebecca walking in front holding her handler's stick.

(Northampton Chronicle & Echo)

3. (left) More fun in Gold Street as a camel gives rides to selected members of the public who were brave enough to accept the challenge from its handler on Thursday 3 September 1964. The purpose of the exercise was to advertise Chipperfield's Circus which was appearing at Midsummer Meadow.

(Northampton Chronicle & Echo)

4. (right) Chipperfield's Circus has arrived at Castle Station on Sunday 7 October 1962 and the parade makes its way out of the station yard towards Black Lion Hill and the town centre, past the crowds of people who have turned out to see the spectacle. On the vehicle is the cannon for projecting the 'Human Cannon Ball' into the air, and following up are two 'Ships of the Desert' and their riders. *(Northampton Chronicle & Echo)*

5. The Boys' Brigade Diamond Jubilee Parade enters Wood Hill from Mercers Row, with members saluting the War Memorial as they march past on Sunday 15 May 1960. They are heading for the Town Hall where Lord Maclay, National President of the Boys' Brigade, is waiting to take the salute. In the background are the once familiar landmarks at the top of the Market Square. *(Northampton Chronicle & Echo)*

6. A band from the Boys' Brigade prepares to leave Queensgrove Methodist Church in Grove Road on Friday 12 April 1963 to head the Kingsley Procession of Witness along the Kettering Road. On the corner of Alcombe Road stands the 'Essoldo' cinema, originally the 'Vaudeville Electric', which opened in 1920 and closed in 1929. After reconstruction it reopened as the 'Regal Super' in March 1930, changing to the 'Essoldo' from March 1956 until August 1968. The main use after then was as a bingo hall, and more recently as a roller-disco.

(Northampton Chronicle & Echo)

7. The Boys' Brigade band is in full swing as they head a huge contingent along Main Road, Duston, on Sunday 15 July 1962. The special occasion is the presentation of the battalion colours to the 11th (Duston Congregational Church) Company. Unfortunately, judging by the spectators' clothing, it does not seem to be a very special day weatherwise for the middle of summer.

(Northampton Chronicle & Echo)

8. Sunday 19 May 1963 was an important day for the Boys' Brigade movement in Northampton, as this gathering shows, for they were attending the stone laying ceremony of the new Northampton Divisional Training Centre and Headquarters on the Mayor Hold. All the buildings in the background were demolished in the early 1970s when the area was redeveloped. *(Northampton Chronicle & Echo)*

9. The gathered assembly of youth organisations and members of Northampton Grammar School for Boys in Billing Road stand in silence as the School Standard is raised during the annual Founders' Day service during the morning of Friday 1 June 1962. Boys who were members of uniformed organisations were required to attend in uniform. The Founders' Day service was introduced in 1955 on the 414th anniversary, the school having been founded on 1 June 1541.

(Northampton Chronicle & Echo)

10. Over 250 Scouts, Cubs and Old Scouts formed up in Abington Park along with the Girl Guides for the St George's Day parade on Sunday 25 April 1965. Here we see the procession heading along Christchurch Road for Christchurch where the St George's Day service was to be held.
(Northampton Chronicle & Echo)

11. On Sunday 11 June 1967, the Annual Parade of Youth Organisations is well under way as a contingent of the Girls' Brigade passes the Town Hall where the Deputy Mayor Mrs Grace Brown takes the salute. The parade and service at All Saints Church was attended by the Boy Scouts, Red Cross, St John Ambulance, Girl Guides, Salvation Army, Church Lads' Brigade, Sea Cadets, Girls' Brigade and Boys' Brigade.

(Northampton Chronicle & Echo)

12. It is Queen Elizabeth II's Coronation Day on Tuesday 2 June 1953, and to commemorate the occasion the town held a Divine Service on the Market Square and a Service Parade that marched past the Town Hall, for which the Deputy Mayor, Alderman Percy Adams, was in attendance to take the salute. In raincoat weather, a group of ex-servicemen file past followed by two of the early style of motorised invalid carriages whose occupants appear to be at risk from inhaling their own exhaust fumes.

(Northampton Chronicle & Echo)

13. An imposing parade of detachments of the Naval, Military, Air and Civil forces attended the opening ceremony of the 'Wings for Victory' week on the Market Square, held from 7 to 15 May 1943. On display in the foreground is a Wellington bomber 'F for Freddie' the star of the film *Target for Tonight* and with 57 bombing raids to its credit. The Tiger Moth training plane included in the display is dwarfed in size in comparison with the twin-engined bomber. *(A. J. Bennett collection)*

14. Also at the opening ceremony for 'Wings for Victory' week, there was the rather unusual sight for that time of a contingent of U.S. coloured troops on parade who are being inspected by the Lord Lieutenant (the Marquess of Exeter) and Northampton's Mayor, Alderman W. Lees. The aim of the exercise was to raise money through the sale of National Savings War Bonds, Certificates or Stamps to fund the manufacture of more Lancasters and Spitfires for the war effort. *(A. J. Bennett collection)*

15. At Wood Hill, on the dismal wet Sunday of 15 July 1962, the Duchess of Gloucester inspects a detachment of the 4th/5th Battalion Northamptonshire Regiment T.A., the last time the colours of the 1st Battalion Northamptonshire Regiment (48th Regiment of foot) were carried aloft before being laid up in the Church of the Holy Sepulchre. Accompanying the Duchess is Earl Spencer (Lord Lieutenant of Northamptonshire). *(Northampton Chronicle & Echo)*

16. Fifty members of the Royal Air Force Association marched in the Battle of Britain parade headed by the band of No. 5 Squadron Air Training Corps on Sunday 19 September 1965. In this scene after the arrival at All Saints Church, Squadron Leader J. F. Sexton lays a wreath at the Cenotaph which is flanked at the four corners by cadets with reversed arms. *(Northampton Chronicle & Echo)*

17. A colourful display of pomp and ceremony in Northampton on Tuesday 25 September 1962 as the Inkerman Company of the Grenadier Guards march from The Drapery into Mercers Row. They were in the town on a recruitment drive and gave an exhibition of Changing the Guard in front of the All Saints Church portico. *(Northampton Chronicle & Echo)*

18. A very pleasant Tuesday 24 July 1962 on the Market Square. The Army was on a recruitment drive, setting up a display and entertaining the people of Northampton with a concert given by the band of the Army Corps. *(Northampton Chronicle & Echo)*

19. The annual Mayor Making ceremony takes place at the Town Hall every May. Here, in the Council Chamber, Alderman J. V. Collier is installed as Mayor for the coming year on Thursday 27 May 1954 in the presence of invited family and guests. The outgoing Mayor, Alderman W. A. Pickering sits on Alderman Collier's left. The attractive sets of overhead lamps have unfortunately since been replaced.

(Northampton Chronicle & Echo)

20. On the first Sunday after Mayor Making, a Civic Sunday Service is held in the town. Here, the parade sets off on 27 May 1962 along St Giles Street towards St Giles Church where the service was to be held. The Town Clerk leads the Mayor's Sergeant (carrying the mace). They are followed by the new Mayor, Councillor E. F. Tompkins and the ex-Mayor Mrs K. M. Gibbs, followed by the Lady Mayoress and other dignitaries.

(Northampton Chronicle & Echo)

21. After St Katherine's Church was demolished, the area was made into a garden of rest and called Memorial Square in memory of those townsfolk who fell during times of conflict. After the opening ceremony during the third week in September 1951, the Marquess of Exeter and the Mayor (Councillor Frank Lee) make their way past the gathering of spectators, followed by Lady Exeter and the Lady Mayoress.

(Northampton Chronicle & Echo)

22. Disgruntled unemployed youths decided to hold a march against unemployment through the town on Saturday 6 April 1963, starting at the Employment Exchange and finishing with an open-air public meeting in Becket's Park. Over 150 people promised to attend, but only 16 turned up, and they are seen making their way from The Mounts into Abington Street en route to Becket's Park. Owing to the small number of people, the meeting was cancelled. *(Northampton Chronicle & Echo)*

23. The annual carnival parade sets out once more on its journey round the town from its Midsummer Meadow starting point on Thursday 15 June 1967. As usual the people of Northampton have turned out in force to witness the spectacle and throw their money into the hundreds of collecting buckets that will pass by, the elevated section of Becket's Park on the Bedford Road being a particularly good vantage point.

(Northampton Chronicle & Echo)

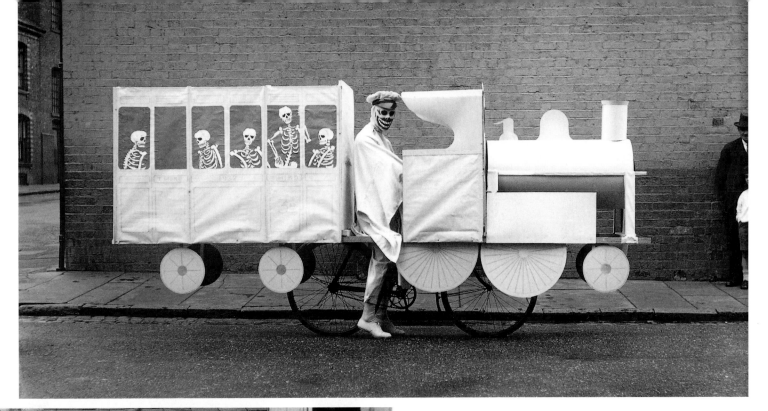

24. (above) The forerunner of the Carnival was called the Cycle Parade, which started in 1890, and here we have two entrants who have kept up the tradition of using bicycles. This picture shows a 1932 entry – 'Ghost Train' – from Mr Groome. *(Robert Wharton collection)*

25. (left) This shows a more traditional entry from earlier years of a bicycle and rider posing for the camera. Nowadays, we might question the rider's gender, but she looks remarkably like 'Klinger' from the television programme 'M.A.S.H.' who frequently dressed up in women's clothes in an effort to get discharged from the forces.

(Robert Wharton collection)

26. A human grandfather clock, winner of first prize in its class, proves the adage that time flies as it hurries down Wellingborough Road just south of Stimpson Avenue during an early 1930s parade. Most people's eyes, however, are on the following attractions, one of which is Mickey Mouse, seen scurrying just behind the clock.   *(Robert Wharton collection)*

27. By the 1950s, the carnival parade included many more mechanised transport displays, one of which was this Bedford OB as an anarchic school bus entry on a 'St Trinians' theme from the Rushden Query Motor Club, but called 'St Querians'. Ideas for carnivals stay much the same for the current generation! Over the years, the route of the parade round the town has been altered, and it is seen here in Military Road during the late 1950s.

(Les Hanson)

AROUND
THE SHOPS

Abington Street has always been very popular
with shoppers, but probably few realise that years
ago it was a largely residential area with no shops
at all! Gradually houses were adapted or rebuilt as
shops, offices and other business establishments,
and in March 1960 the last private house was sold
off. In more recent times, even such non-
residential sites as the New Theatre succumbed
to the shop developer's quest for property,
demolished to make way for a new Fine Fare
supermarket. It is hardly likely that anyone will
protest at a loss of architectural heritage when
that building's turn for demolition comes round.
In 1979, the demolition of the Notre Dame High
School together with its chapel was highly
controversial, and was replaced with another
concrete block of shops.

28. This shows a typical 1950s view of Abington
Street with the New Theatre still in its
dominating position on the right, with its four
stone finials on top of the building. The date is
Monday 16 November 1959 and the Christmas
decorations are in place ready for the big switch-
on of the lights. There is still two-way traffic and
pedestrianisation is many years away.
(Northampton Chronicle & Echo)

29. (left) This continues the 1950s theme in 1953, with shoppers streaming past two long-established shops, Kendall's Umbrella store on the corner of Fish Street and British Home Stores on the opposite side of the street.

(Northampton Chronicle & Echo)

30. (right) This view from 19 November 1962 shows a change in clothes fashion, but the same volume of shoppers. This is looking down Abington Street towards Mercers Row in the days when buses actually stopped outside the shops, making it easier for shoppers to travel home with all their shopping. Crossing the road, however, was another matter!   *(Northampton Chronicle & Echo)*

31. A successful experiment by the Northampton Abington Street Traders' Association to attract people to Abington Street by organising a spectacular Christmas lights display in 1959, set the trend for the following years. The scheme was unique in the East Midlands, and, as sightseers and shoppers increased, so did sales, and Abington Street became one of the foremost centres for shopping in this part of the country. This picture, taken on Monday 28 November 1960 from outside Notre Dame High School, shows the Christmas lights shining brightly above the busy Abington Street.

(Northampton Chronicle & Echo)

32. With the Market Square on the left, this shows Abington Street on the afternoon of a very busy Saturday in January 1962 with many shoppers in for the sales. It is interesting to relate the prices of various items from this period. A new Morris 1000 cost £675; A three-piece suite £50; a Philips stereo radiogram 70 guineas; a Bush 17" black-and-white television 65 guineas; a vacuum cleaner £18; a bottle of Scotch whisky £2; and a pack of 100 Senior Service £1. For food, a 2 lb bag of sugar was one shilling, and a pint of milk eightpence (8d). A bag of ready-salted crisps was threepence (3d), while the only flavoured variety at the time, cheese and onion, was a penny (1d) more a bag. *(Northampton Chronicle & Echo)*

33. An intriguing look inside Kingham's Store in Abington Street on Tuesday 22 November 1960 shows the shelves well stocked with just over a month to go before Christmas. A wide range of Christmas crackers can be seen, together with traditional boxes of shortbread biscuits and gift boxes of chocolates. Established in 1834, Kingham's first appeared in Abington Street in 1885, at No. 8, and expanded to include Nos. 10 and 12. In 1959, James Brothers took over the business, but still traded under the name of Kingham's. The shop was well known for its sale of specialised teas and roasted coffees, and to many shoppers the aroma of coffee within the shop will be a lasting memory. When the shop finally closed in 1963 it was a sad loss to the shoppers and to Northampton. But, as is the case with many long-established or family businesses, they cannot run on sentiment for the good of the public, and if customers desert them for their everyday purchases they cannot be expected to be there when the customer needs something out of the ordinary. *(Northampton Chronicle & Echo)*

34. A look inside Brierley's store in Gold Street during the autumn of 1963, showing none other than the owner Frank Brierley tempting his loyal customers with one of the many bargains in the store. A familiar figure within his store, he would often revert to his market stall days and have instant sales, making his customers offers they could not refuse, which had the advantage that they came back again. The store stocked a wide range of products at knock-down-prices. You never knew what you would find next, but it would be cheap. At this time, he had a light bulb for a shilling, a tin of Nescafé coffee for two shillings, and even 20 Woodbines for 3/5d. Frank later retired and his daughter ran the business.

(Northampton Chronicle & Echo)

35. Bridge Street in about 1915, and an electric tram rumbles down the hill towards Far Cotton. Outside the shops of Crane's (saddler) and Crick's (cooper) a shopkeeper sweeps the path without offering a glance. Up until October 1914, the trams to Far Cotton continued to be horse-drawn, before the electric ones took over; even these ended in December 1934. Across the road, a lady shopper looks at one of the window displays, while her children play on the path. They must be hoping for the chance to go into Clarke's sweet shop opposite before going home.   *(E. C. Lloyd collection)*

36. Children have always loved sweets and sweet shops and will continue to do so. Here is a typical scene in a Northampton sweet shop on Saturday 6 February 1960, and a couple of very well-dressed sisters are purchasing a bag of sweets. The range of products in the glass cabinets is fascinating and varied and the girls must have really enjoyed looking and being tempted by each item !

(Northampton Chronicle & Echo)

37. (right) The classic corner shop, so familiar for many years, proved invaluable in the days before the supermarkets took hold. Situated in residential areas, the corner shops were handy and convenient and had an amazing range of products. This picture, taken on Thursday 25 August 1960, shows Mr. Geddes shop in Ecton Street at the junction of Victoria Road, not far from Abington Square. The building still survives today as a private residence. *(Northampton Chronicle & Echo)*

38. (left) A nostalgic look along Kettering Road towards the Unitarian Church and Abington Square, before the buildings on the left side were demolished, taking with them many familiar shop names. Many will remember Robinson's television and radio dealer from this photograph taken on Thursday 24 June 1971.

(Northampton Borough Council)

39. A miserable wet day on 13 January 1989 keeps most shoppers at home, but time is running out for this row of five shops in St Giles Square. A café, picture gallery, woollens shop, and boutique make up four of them, but the most memorable one to disappear is Lawes & Sons, the cycle shop on the corner. The cycle shop has existed on this site since the turn of the century and another part of Northampton's character and history would be demolished with the building. Not all is lost, however, as the two-storey Victorian building hidden behind the shop frontages will be renovated and become a tourist and visitors' centre for the town.

(Northampton Chronicle & Echo)

40. The Co-op arcade is busy with shoppers in this picture taken during February 1964. This view, looking towards Abington Street from The Riding, changed very little until recent years, and the licensed restaurant on the first floor was a popular venue for shoppers in Northampton. The Co-operative building opened in 1905, with the arcade opening in 1938, and although the front portion remained unmodernised, the rest was rebuilt. The arcade still exists and is used regularly by shoppers and as a short cut between Abington Street and St Giles Street.

(Northampton Chronicle & Echo)

41. Bus passengers at the 'Green' bus station in Derngate on Tuesday 16 April 1963 queue at the teashop to take refreshment before their journey. Many Northamptonians will remember the scene here, and this was one of the many memorable aspects of town life that would disappear when the Derngate Bus Station closed. *(Northampton Chronicle & Echo)*

42. Saturday afternoon shoppers on the Market Square gather round and mingle with the autograph hunters and fans of the Beverley Sisters on 20 October 1951 outside Abel's music and record store. Having appeared on stage all week at the New Theatre, the Beverley Sisters were invited to Abel's store to autograph records and sheet music. Since their first music hall engagement in August 1945 at the Croydon Empire, the Beverley sisters rapidly rose to the top of their business and by this time were Britain's leading girl vocalist trio. Their records such as 'Teasin' and 'Hurry Home to Me' were top favourites and the sisters appeared at the London Palladium and performed overseas. At the time of writing, they are still, incredibly, a major act.

(Northampton Chronicle & Echo)

43. (left) The small shops in the Emporium Arcade were a great attraction to shoppers. Standing on the Market Square between Abel's record store and the *Chronicle & Echo* building, it led through to Newland. Here, on Friday 26 April 1968, there is the opportunity to preview a new shop which is to open the next day. The Northampton-shire Association for Mental Health is opening up a 'nearly new' shop to raise funds.

(Northampton Chronicle & Echo)

44. (right) The patron of the Association then was Lady Spencer, and she is seen talking to the management at the official opening on the Saturday. It was the first such shop she had opened. Sadly, by the end of 1971 all shops ceased trading in the Arcade, and, amid much controversy, the building was demolished the next year.

(Northampton Chronicle & Echo)

45. Rochelle Lofting, apparently recognised at the time as Britain's most photographed model, was in Northampton during the second week of May 1957, appearing in a production called 'Glamour Girl' at the New Theatre. Rochelle, whose vital statistics were 42-23-36, visited the Midland Carpet Company's showrooms in Sheep Street during her stay. She is seen here receiving helpful advice from the shop manager, Mr Kirby, who seems to have temporarily lost interest in his merchandise, as she examines a £30 Wilton carpet, one of the hundreds on display. She was in the process of furnishing her new home in Chiswick, London.

(Northampton Chronicle & Echo)

46. People cram into Currys Store in Abington Street on Tuesday 11 April 1967 to get a glimpse of top disc jockey and TV personality Pete Murray. A recording session for Radio Luxembourg was being staged, due to be broadcast on 28 April, and one lucky lady succeeds in getting a kiss from the star, while autograph hunters await their turn. During the programme, prizes were given away and record requests taken.

(Northampton Chronicle & Echo)

47. It is market day at Northampton on Wednesday 16 January 1963 and the traders are out in force regardless of the atrocious weather conditions. A full-scale blizzard has set in and, judging by the handful of people in the picture, most must have gone home, and no doubt the traders will shortly be off too. The 1962-3 winter must have been a trying time for all market traders as the snow lingered through to the spring. And who would have thought of taking a photograph in these conditions, and getting such a telling picture ? *(Northampton Chronicle & Echo)*

48. In complete contrast to the picture on the previous page, this was photographed on 24 June 1971 in the height of summer. No doubt strawberries, cherries and other seasonal products are selling well. However, in the background, things are far from happy. The hands from the clock above the Emporium Arcade are missing, and this gives the secret away. The place is about to close with the many little shops having to cease trading. In fact, within six months, demolition would start and another landmark would disappear. Even Abel's Records had closed in 1970. Many Northamptonians will remember the hours of joy that they had listening to records in the row of booths inside the shop.

(Northampton Borough Council)

49. The Market Square dates back to 1235 and has provided shoppers centuries of shopping opportunities. Situated in the heart of the town, it is easily accessible and over the years, the types of products sold have been numerous and varied. In this picture, a butcher, Mr Frost from Hardingstone, sells his meat to an eager customer who will look forward to enjoying the joint on Sunday. This 1930s view shows that all the nearby stalls are also selling meat. *(Robert Wharton collection)*

50. (right) A number of traders selling fruit and vegetables would set up their stalls on days other than market days. In this photograph on Tuesday 25 August 1964, the warm sunny weather has brought out the mums and tots amongst others. Here we see a little girl buying a pound of tomatoes. It is interesting to note the prices of the day – pears are 9d a lb., four peaches for a shilling, a whole cucumber for 1/4d, and four oranges for a shilling. Those were the days!!

(Northampton Chronicle & Echo)

51. (left) This photograph from Christmas Eve 1966 shows many last-minute Christmas shoppers queuing to buy mistletoe for celebrations later. Obviously the rain hasn't dampened their spirits, and even the trader whose stall has no cover can raise a smile as he gets wetter and wetter.

(Northampton Chronicle & Echo)

ALONG THE HIGHWAYS

52. Any building around the town centre with a blank bricked end was a prime advertising site during the 1930s especially for the local theatres and cinemas of the town. This view looking down St Giles Street from the corner of Castilian Street on Thursday 7 August 1930 was to change considerably over the next few years. The shape of things to come can be seen in the General Post Office building constructed during 1917 and set back ready for road widening. *(W. J. S. Meredith)*

Posters have been a familiar sight around the town over the years. In the past, they would decorate any piece of spare wall, fencing, or the end of buildings, as money could be made by renting advertising space, especially in prime positions. In later years however, tighter controls were placed on advertisers, limiting them to the use of properly constructed hoardings usually around a piece of spare land which would otherwise become an overgrown eyesore or dumping ground.

As time goes by, these posters themselves become of interest, as the selection on these pages shows.

53. (above) A section of the hoarding at the bottom of Newland on Wednesday 19 April 1939 while work is in progress on the *Chronicle & Echo* building. The car obviously belongs to a 'rep' as the radiator and back window advertise State Express cigarettes.
(*Northampton Chronicle & Echo*)

54. (left) Work on the hoarding at the bottom of Newland gets under way in November 1938.
(*Northampton Chronicle & Echo*)

55. (left) Advertisement hoarding in St John Street opposite the station on Tuesday 22 February 1938 which includes a poster advertising the British Industries Fair at Birmingham.
(W. J. S. Meredith)

56. (below) The large hoarding on the corner of Balmoral Road and Queens Park Parade held many posters as in this January 1954 view.
(Northampton Chronicle & Echo)

57. (left) Posters on the hoarding fronting the site of the proposed new St Peter's Parish Hall in Marefair on Friday 29 August 1930. *(W. J. S. Meredith)*

58. (above) A selection of posters neatly placed on a house at the end of Weston Street on Monday 3 May 1937. The 'Loyal Greetings' poster refers to the forthcoming coronation of King George VI on 12 May. *(W. J. S. Meredith)*

59. Demolition work begins in earnest in Abington Street between Fish Street and Dychurch Lane on Tuesday 15 February 1938 as another row of old shops bites the dust. A man watches proceedings while taking a rest from pushing his handcart, a conveyance once common around the streets of Northampton.   *(W. J. S. Meredith)*

60. A view along Fish Street later in the year on Monday 17 October 1938 and the demolition of 32 Abington Street (seen in the previous photograph) is well under way, soon to be followed by the building on the left. On the other side of Abington Street are the buildings in Wood Street, later to be demolished to provide the entrance for the Grosvenor Centre, leaving only the street name-plate as evidence. *(W. J. S. Meredith)*

61. A busy scene in The Drapery during the latter half of 1927 shows the increasing presence of the motor car in place of the pony and trap for transporting the more affluent people to do their shopping. The majority of townsfolk, however, still used to rely on the tram, and here No. 28 picks up a passenger en route to Kingsthorpe. The fine architecture of the buildings particularly on the left side of the Drapery is evident.

62. A moment in time from the past has been captured in this photograph looking down Abington Street towards the town centre in the summer of 1906. As a hansom cab disappears into the distance, tram car No. 8 heads for the County Cricket Ground while on the left is a horse-drawn wagon, and boys making deliveries from a handcart. People in the street are inquisitive of the cameraman, including the attractive young woman peering out from Mansell's (electrical engineers) doorway on the left. Also of interest are the external gas lamps for lighting up the shop windows of Slade's (booksellers) and Partridge's. *(Robert Wharton collection)*

63. On Thursday 16 April 1931, work was being carried out on the Exchange Cinema in the Parade, which was showing Al Jolson's *Mammy* with 'scenes in colour'. Twenty months earlier, this same cinema had shown the first 'talkie' in town with *The Singing Fool*. The cinema was renamed the Gaumont in April 1950 and the Odeon in March 1964, eventually closing as a cinema in September 1974, later to re-open as a luxury Bingo club. The building behind and to the right of the tram was demolished during September 1938 and was replaced by the 'Fish Market'.

(W. J. S. Meredith)

64. (right) The Wellingborough Road as seen on Friday 18 November 1960. Bollards are being installed in the road outside the Plaza cinema to aid pedestrians in crossing the busy road, and a postman rides by on his bicycle, with a Bedford van alongside and an Albion behind. The Plaza had a number of different names over the years, including the Picture Palace, King's Gaiety and Prince of Wales, becoming the Plaza in about 1931 until July 1969, by which time it was both a cinema and bingo hall. *(Northampton Chronicle & Echo)*

65. (below) This view from West Bridge of the cinema on the corner of St James Park Road was taken in September 1936 while the cinema was being refurbished. Since about 1920 it had been called the St James Electric cinema until being sold and closed in August 1936, reopening in November 1936 as the Roxy. The Roxy closed in July 1949 and the building became part of Dover's cycle accessories factory, eventually being demolished in the early 1970s. *(W. J. S. Meredith)*

66. St James End about 1910, when the pace of life was much slower than it is today and the sight of a camera still attracted a good deal of attention. As the horse-drawn carts go about their daily business on this summer's day, tram car No. 17 works steadily towards the town centre and its destination at 'Kingsley Park', somewhat lacking in passengers at this stage of the journey. The electric trams began on this route in 1904, and it was the last to operate when trams were withdrawn from the town, the final tram running on 15 December 1934. *(E. C. Lloyd collection)*

67. When the trams were withdrawn from service, they were stripped and the bodies sold off. Here, outside the depot at St James on Sunday 1 September 1935, things are not quite what they seem on the scrap line. Car No. 22 has had its upper deck removed, car No. 19 has had its upper deck and truck removed and been loaded on to a cart ready for the horse to take away, but car No. 21 is still substantially complete. Originally called 'Northampton Corporation Tramways', the name was later altered to 'Northampton Corporation Transport'. *(W. J. S. Meredith)*

68. In a scene at the Mayor Hold on Sunday 26 May 1928, a driver cranks the handle to start the engine of his Leyland Lion bus which looks very modern compared to the two ancient Daimlers on the right with their solid tyres and very little protection for their drivers. The Northampton Motor Omnibus Company Ltd was started by J. Grose Ltd (motor engineers) in July 1914, running daily services to a number of outlying villages and small towns from Northampton. Later in the year that this photograph was taken (1928), the bus franchise was sold to the United Counties Omnibus Company. Grose's remain in business to this day. *(W. J. S. Meredith)*

69. It was an overcast and dismal day on Wednesday 16 February 1938, brightened slightly for the photographer by the interesting array of buses parked on land bounded by Victoria Promenade and Bridge Street. Behind the buses is the old Phoenix Brewery built in 1856, becoming the Northampton Brewery Co. in 1874 and remaining independent until merging with Phipps' Brewery in 1957. Adjacent to the brewery at this time stood an animal feed and corn merchant's premises (behind the gas lamp). *(W. J. S. Meredith)*

70. An intriguing scene along Barrack Road circa 1906 finds horse power very much in evidence as in the foreground a horse and dray from Phipps Brewery makes a delivery of barrelled and bottled beer to Edward Dunkley, beer retailer. Further along, people go about their business and shopping in their pony-and-traps, while in the distance a 'modern' form of transport in the shape of an electric tram proceeds towards Kingsthorpe.

(E. C. Lloyd collection)

71. (above) Since this photograph of the Welford Road/Harborough Road junction was taken in 1953, all the buildings on the left-hand side, including G. Brookes garage on the corner have passed into history to make way for supermarkets and the like. The driver of the British Railways Dennis van would not now get away with driving along with his vehicle's tailgate down either, and how different is the volume of traffic from nowadays. *(Northampton Chronicle & Echo)*

72. (right) Quite a rural scene of Glan-Y-Mor Terrace on the Harborough Road circa 1912 showing horse and rider progressing gently towards town while one of the new-fangled motor cars passes the premises of J. Rose, Dairy Farmer, who advertises 'new milk delivered twice daily'. *(E. C. Lloyd collection)*

73. So rare was the sight of a motor vehicle in Stimpson Avenue around 1909 that children and the cameraman could stand in the middle of the road while the camera was set up and the glass plate exposed with no risk of getting run over. No doubt some of the children shown here attended Stimpson Avenue School, opened in 1894. *(E. C. Lloyd collection)*

74. Another view in Stimpson Avenue, this time of J. Sears & Co. shoe factory on the corner of Adnitt Road, well known for their 'True-Form' brand name and photographed in 1953, just after being taken over by the Charles Clore empire. Built in 1903, the building was described as a 'manufacturing showpiece' with a floor area of 170,000 square feet in which 1500 people were employed on 150 different processes of footwear production. After being taken over, manufacturing processes were combined with the Manfield shoe factory and the decline started, leading to closure in 1967. Heavily vandalised over the years, the corner section was demolished during December 1980, with the whole site later being used for residential purposes. At this time however, gas lamps still provided the street lighting, while the two boys (one with a suitcase and umbrella!) await the nod from a 'lollipop' man, who was standing on the opposite side of the road, to cross in safety.

(Northampton Chronicle & Echo)

75. Those of you who have Part One of this series of books may recognise this scene, which was taken at the same time as the frontispiece in that volume. They are such a wonderful pair of pictures that we thought that we should include the second for your enjoyment. This was taken on Thursday 2 August 1962 in St James Square, off St James Street. Children play 'leap frog' watched by an even younger generation and the cul-de-sac cowboy who has an incredibly long barrel to his 'six-shooter'. Two of the boys are from the Cosby family whose Mum and Dad rented No. 1 St James Square, for which at that time they paid 9s 3d per week.

(Northampton Chronicle & Echo)

76. One of the forerunners of the modern 'pedestrian areas', or what was then referred to as 'slums', this view down Alliston Gardens off the Barrack Road shows one of the few paved areas between rows of houses that existed in Northampton apart from St James Square. Photographed after a light snowfall on Monday 15 November 1965 looking down towards Semilong Road, a good number of the houses are still occupied, although they were all demolished twelve months later.

(Northampton Chronicle & Echo)

77. Another old part of Northampton off the Barrack Road was the narrow streets of the impressively named Marble Arch and Temple Bar, the latter of which is seen here on Thursday 6 October 1960. One of the few exposed cobbled streets remaining in the town, although the right hand side is still standing, it has now passed into history, along with the lady heading towards Maple Street with her shopping. Adam Faith, advertised on the middle poster as appearing at the ABC Northampton, proved to be more durable! *(Northampton Chronicle & Echo)*

78. It was a rather wet and dismal Christmas Eve Thursday in December 1964, especially apparent in this view looking from Portland Street towards the Wellingborough Road. The wall in front of St Edmunds Church was demolished and a new wall built nearer the church during the road widening scheme in 1967. This was followed by the demolition of the church itself in 1979. *(Northampton Chronicle & Echo)*

79. The members of the 'Invicta Cycling Club' have certainly gained the attention of Saturday shoppers as they cycle around the town on 24 October 1953 promoting road safety by giving demonstrations on how not to ride a bike. Here they are shown on old bicycles being typically inconsiderate to other road users in Abington Street.

(Northampton Chronicle & Echo)

80. The traffic even in those days seems to have been heavy, and one hopes that their demonstrations of dangerous riding did not cause themselves any accidents. Here they are riding round the Gold Street/Bridge Street junction in front of All Saints Church. It is interesting to note the style of 1950s clothes and hair styles of the onlookers. Not many years before, all the men would have been wearing hats or caps, but now only a few caps survive. *(Northampton Chronicle & Echo)*

81. (left) A scene in Marefair which shows to good effect the various styles of buildings that used to be on the north side prior to demolition, to make way for the building of Barclaycard House. In this view, taken on Tuesday 6 September 1966, the buildings stand forlornly waiting for the day when the bulldozers arrive. Just past the garage is the narrow entrance to Pike Lane, leading through to Castle Street.

(Northampton Chronicle & Echo)

82. (below) In marked contrast to the previous picture, this shows Marefair when it was a busy thoroughfare, being the main access into the town centre from the St James direction, and traffic jams frequently built up during rush hours. Photographed in the morning of Tuesday 28 March 1961, it was two days prior to the opening of the new St Peters Way, which probably was a factor in the decline of Gold Street and Marefair as shopping areas.

(Northampton Chronicle & Echo)

83. This elevated view of Marefair in September 1954 shows the shops and the 'North Western Hotel' still very much in use, with a British Road Services Leyland Beaver about to drive off. At this time not so many people owned cars, and commuters (then known as season ticket holders) would often walk between the Castle station and the town centre, with the shops picking up passing trade from them as a consequence. Once a common sight everywhere was the strip pressure pads seen on the road outside the hotel which triggered the operation of the traffic lights, which now would be replaced by an metal-sensitive loop under the road surface.

(Northampton Chronicle & Echo)

84. A glimpse down Lower Mounts on Thursday 24 September 1964 finds United Counties Bristol Lodekka service 312 heading for Pitsford as people pass the time of day under the road sign which reminds us that the A45 once went straight through the centre of Northampton. All the buildings on the left side were later demolished to make way for road widening and car parking facilities. Amongst businesses lost was the 'Bombay Restaurant', a popular place to round off a Friday or Saturday evening 'out on the town' during the late 50s and early 60s.

(Northampton Chronicle & Echo)

85. The 'Franklins Guildhall Hotel' in Guildhall Road is shown as up for sale in August 1954, bringing an end to an era. It had gained a reputation for fine cuisine and had been host to many businessmen and farmers for nearly a century. The hotel finally closed on Saturday 30 October 1954, having been purchased by Northamptonshire County Council for use as offices, the ground floor later being occupied by the 'Northamptonshire Countryside Centre'. There is an interesting collecting of cars – on the left is a Morris 10, with behind it a Standard and Vauxhall Wyvern, and on the right is a Singer, then an ex-army Austin Tilley, and a Hillman.

(Northampton Chronicle & Echo)

86. On the Market Square, Northampton Corporation workmen raise the copper ball towards the top of the Fountain on Monday 30 August 1954, the last time it received a face-lift. The ornate cast ironwork is shown to good advantage, but what is also interesting is the statement on the plaque, the first part of which reads: 'Presented to the Mayor and Corporation in Trust for the Inhabitants of Northampton', a request that obviously fell on deaf ears.

(Northampton Chronicle & Echo)

87. (right) Northampton Corporation planned a set of roadworks around the town centre for a three-day period in March 1960, imaginatively called 'Operation Road-Up', which caused absolute mayhem to the traffic, although it was all well planned. Here in Wood Hill on Wednesday 23 March, it's all systems go as, to the rattle of jack-hammers, the old tarmac and granite sets are removed by a Carrier Bantam (on the left) and a Commer Superpoise in preparation for the new road material.

(Northampton Chronicle & Echo)

88. (left) A number of people spent their daily working lives on the streets of Northampton. At The Parade on the Market Square, a council workman takes time to buy a poppy from Tony Pamment while levelling up the paving slabs on Saturday morning 7 November 1953.

(Northampton Chronicle & Echo)

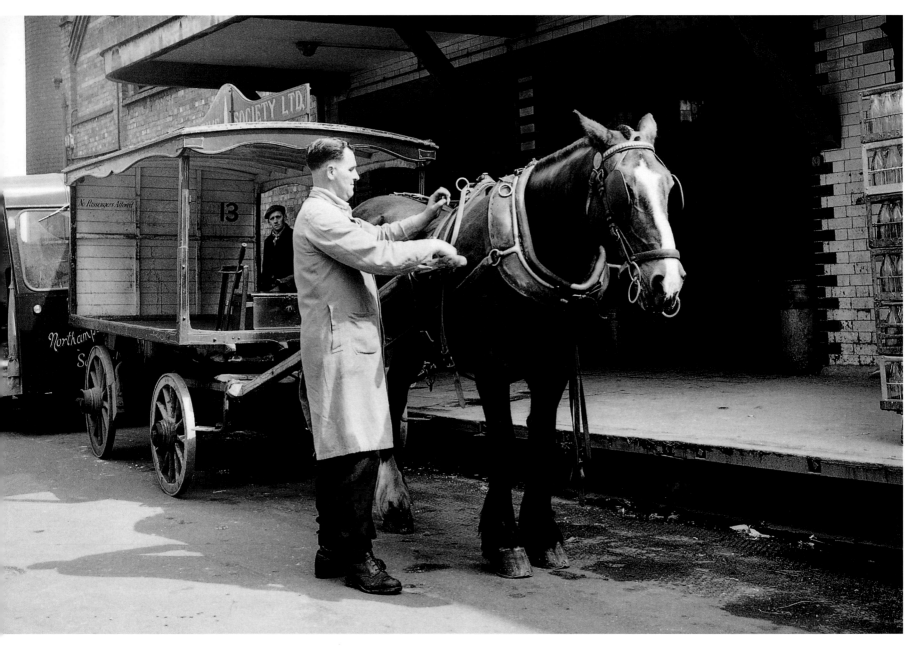

89. By May 1962, out of fifty-seven 'milk floats' operated by the Co-operative Society, only thirteen remained pulled by horses, and people waking up to the sound of the brittle tattoo of horses' hooves on the street outside, while their morning 'pinta' was being delivered, was fast becoming a thing of the past. One of these combinations is seen here at the Ransome Road depot on Wednesday 9 May. It was here that the horses lived in stables on the first floor above a garage overlooking the railway.

(Northampton Chronicle & Echo)

90. At the General Post Office on Friday 10 September 1954, the arrival of a new 'Electruc' electrically driven handcart for delivering parcels created a good deal of interest, for it was a great improvement on the wicker parcels handcart which it was replacing. If it was perhaps not quite so manoeuvrable, it wasn't half so much 'hard graft'.

(Northampton Chronicle & Echo)

91. January 1963 brought some very hostile winter weather with snow and prolonged spells of frost throughout the day as well as the night. In this view from Spencer Bridge Road on a very bleak Thursday 17 January, looking across the railway coal yard and the town, billowing clouds of steam and smoke can be seen emanating from the power station at Nunn Mills, as they endeavour to keep up with the demand for electricity.

(Northampton Chronicle & Echo)

92. Overwhelmed by the twelve-storey blocks of flats of Beaumont Court and Claremont Court, this old building on the corner of The Mayor Hold and Scarletwell Street remains as a reminder of a more pleasing style of architecture in this wintry scene on Wednesday 23 January 1963. In use as a café when this photograph was taken, it previously had a more salubrious past as 'The Old Jolly Smokers' public house. Unfortunately, the building was demolished in the Mayor Hold redevelopment, but amazingly the short row of terraced houses between it and the flats survived.

(Northampton Chronicle & Echo)

93. Another contrast of old and new on Saturday 22 September 1979 as the stark lines of 'Northampton House' tower above part of the Notre Dame building, whose graceful lines and curves are still evident even in this state of demolition. Shoppers are making their way along Abington Street without even glancing at what's happening to their town.

(Northampton Chronicle & Echo)

94. The first scheme for extending the Town Hall thought up by the Borough Architect's Department is seen here in model form on Thursday 29 November 1962, being enthusiastically surveyed by Alderman T. H. Cockerill (centre), Leonard Howarth (Borough Architect), and Mr J. Robotham (Senior Assistant Architect). This is a stark design, typical of the 1960s era, with a preponderance of concrete and glass and with little or no thought given to its impact on the surrounding area. Thank goodness it was never built. At least the new Town Hall extension now built is in keeping with the existing architecture and is a credit to its designers. If such plans could seriously be considered in the 1960s, we must be grateful that more of our historic town was not destroyed.

(Northampton Chronicle & Echo)

95. The car in front is a Lanchester, followed by a Vauxhall, weaving around the piles of slushy snow in Abington Street during the winter of 1947. With record low temperatures and heavy snowfall, the January to March 1947 period was most memorable. Northampton Borough Council, being unable to cope with the large amount of snow, obtained the help of the military to clear the main streets in the town. Amazingly, the winter ended in dramatic style, with gales and mild weather to melt all the snow and create flood conditions. *(Northampton Chronicle & Echo)*

96. A sea of water greets drivers in Mill Lane, Kingsthorpe on Sunday 14 January 1979 and as usual a number have tried to drive through the water, got stuck, and have had to abandon their vehicles. Astonishingly, a figure is still sitting in this Ford Capri, which is complete with furry dashboard. The River Nene at this location between Kings Heath and Kingsthorpe regularly flooded, and on this occasion heavy snow followed by rain and a rapid thaw caused the Nene to burst its banks. No doubt this picture will bring memories flooding back for folk who lived in this area of the town. *(Northampton Chronicle & Echo)*

97. The winter of 1962-3 was one of the most severe in recent years. Heavy snow started falling on Boxing Day 1962, and this started a ten week period of exceptionally severe frost and heavy snow falls. The emergency services were out in force throughout this period and the following pictures show some of the efforts put in to help the situation. A heavy snowfall on the night of 19 January 1963 caused the Northampton Corporation snowplough, a Dennis Pax, to be kept particularly busy. It is seen here on Monday 21 January on the Kings Heath Estate, coming up Severn Drive past a pre-war Model 'C' Ford as some of the residents clear away snow from their own paths.

(Northampton Chronicle & Echo)

98. (right) During this particular blizzard, gale-force easterly winds whipped snow onto the roads and railway lines. It set in early in the evening of 19 January and continued into the early hours of Sunday. Consequently, on the Sunday, railwaymen were out in force trying to clear the six-foot snow drifts on the railway lines. In this picture, photographed at Kingsthorpe Mill, north of Castle station, the snowdrifts are easily visible covering the southbound line from Market Harborough. A freight train has just passed heading towards Northampton.
(Northampton Chronicle & Echo)

99. (left) For the railway enthusiasts, the locomotive in this picture is an ex-L.M.S. Stanier 8F 2-8-0 slowly heading its rake of coal wagons towards Market Harborough. *(Northampton Chronicle & Echo)*

100. The fire brigade was kept extremely busy during one particular extremely cold spell between 18 January and 25 January 1963 when the temperature remained below freezing even during the day. During the night, the temperature plunged to 0°F with 32 degrees of frost, and that is cold!! Consequently, frozen water pipes were widespread throughout the town. The watering facilities at the locomotive shed did not escape, and in this picture we see preparations for the watering up of steam locomotives by the fire brigade on Thursday 24 January 1963.

(Northampton Chronicle & Echo)

101. Whole blocks of houses were frozen in the Kings Heath estate. In fact, one morning about 200 supply pipes had been reported as frozen up for over 24 hours. Emergency water supplies were transported to Kings Heath in milk churns borrowed from the Civil Defence units. This picture shows the firemen hard at work on Thursday 24 January 1963.

(Northampton Chronicle & Echo)

102/103. On 31 December 1969, a freight train broke in half and, when one of the wagons jumped the line, the others piled around it, causing all four lines in Roade Cutting to be blocked. A passenger train, the 11.26 a.m. Northampton to Euston, collided with one of the wagons, and the resulting accident caused the death of the driver of the train and injury to eight passengers. Emergency services were soon called, but the steep cutting sides hampered the rescuers in their task. The fire brigade used oxyacetylene torches and winches to release the driver, while doctors and nurses were delivered to the site by using a trolley as shown in the first picture. Other passengers alighted and walked the half mile along the line to the site of Roade station. Incidentally, the rest of the freight train, including the engine, stopped about half a mile from the scene of the crash. *(both Northampton Chronicle & Echo)*

104. Flames leap 30 feet into the air from the blazing roof of a derelict three-storey warehouse in Greyfriars Street on 17 August 1970. The disused warehouse was formerly used by Associated Wholesale Stationers Ltd, and was on the edge of a clearance area, and probably set alight by children. Hundreds of people crowded around the area as 20 firemen fought for more than an hour to bring the flames under control. Police cordoned off Newland and Wood Street while drifting smoke reduced visibility in Abington Street to a few yards at one stage. The heat was felt one hundred yards away and smoke and flames were visible for miles. Amazingly, while the blaze was at its height, about 400 people were playing bingo in the old Temperance Cinema nearby. Apparently players were only interrupted from their game for a few seconds when the caller broke off to ask what was happening outside.

(Northampton Chronicle & Echo)

105. Northampton fire brigade have been called out to tackle yet another fire in a derelict factory near Abington Square on Friday 16 June 1967. The building, formerly belonging to Wareings (Northampton Footwear) Ltd, in Kettering Road, was due for demolition when the fire broke out. Apparently started by children, flames leapt 30 feet into the air and smoke could be seen from the town centre. Three fire tenders and a Metz turntable accompanied the firemen, and in this picture, the worst of the fire is over, the back wall and roof of the building had caved in, and damping down of the fire was taking place. *(Northampton Chronicle & Echo)*

106. In the evening of Thursday 8 November 1962, Edward C. Cook's warehouse in Lower Mounts caught fire in the basement, and a spectacular blaze resulted which severely damaged the interior of the premises. Forty firemen from Northampton, Earls Barton and Brixworth battled for about an hour to control the blaze. Here, after the flames had subsided, a jet of water is directed into the front of the warehouse to make sure everywhere is dampened down sufficiently. The petrol pumps and tanks must have been a major cause of concern. *(Northampton Chronicle & Echo)*

107. The street scene during the Edward C. Cook fire on 8 November 1962. Fire tenders block the way and water hoses litter the ground like spaghetti as they coil from hydrants to pumps and carry water under high pressure to the firefighters at the front line. At this time, though, the fire had been largely brought under control and things had moved into the damping down phase. *(Northampton Chronicle & Echo)*

108. To enable policemen to control traffic at major junctions and allow pedestrians to cross the road, new press-button traffic light signals were installed. On a wet Thursday 4 April 1963, at the Kingsthorpe Road and Mill Lane junction, near the Cock Hotel, police constable George Hickford ushers pedestrians over the crossing and stands next to the press-button apparatus. These were 'Panda' crossings, which were superseded by the present 'Pelican' crossings. *(Northampton Chronicle & Echo)*

109. A policeman stands in Princess Street (between Newland and Wood Street) and looks at a chimney on fire in a house in Greyfriars Street. It is a still, cold January day in 1960 and the smoke from the chimney spreads across the street creating an atmospheric, and probably very smelly, scene. The building on the right is the Temperance Cinema and the sign shows that the side entrance to gain access to the balcony and back stalls is located nearby. On the opposite side of the street, a glimpse of some motorcycles indicates the location of André Baldet's scooter and autobike shop, keenly eyed by the youth on the right. In years to come, the whole of this area would be cleared and redeveloped.
(Northampton Chronicle & Echo)

110. A wonderful collection of cars on the Market Square on Thursday 3 March 1960. From the left we can see a Ford Anglia, Morris Traveller, Austin 8, Austin A40 Somerset, Morris 8 and Morris Oxford. In the background is the one side of the Market Square that did not suffer in the modernisation programme, and although businesses have changed hands over the years, the buildings have remained. Judging by the number of policemen it looks like a road fund licence purge is going on. This was, of course, in the days before traffic wardens. *(Northampton Chronicle & Echo)*

111. An accident in St James Road, near the junction with St James Mill Road, on Saturday 28 May 1960, shows PC 'Doughy' Sharpe wearing his bike clips, in attendance trying to sort out the problem. A Caterpillar shovel, which was being unloaded from a lorry, came loose and fell into the side of a passing corporation bus. Fortunately, no-one was seriously injured, although three passengers were treated for shock at Northampton General Hospital. The bus depot was only down the road, so it wasn't long before the bus was towed away for repair. The bus is a Crossley DD42/3 from 1946, and it still exists, with efforts being made to rescue it from a Cambridgeshire scrap yard. *(Northampton Chronicle & Echo)*

112. A mishap in St James Road in which sacks of grain, fresh from Heygate's Mill at Bugbrooke, have fallen off a cart which seems to have crashed into a house. From the photograph, which looks towards the town centre, all the houses and the furthest pub on the corner of St James Mill Road have since been demolished for road widening purposes, and only the nearest pub, the Thomas à Becket, survives. In this scene from November 1953, the policeman takes details while a handful of spectators watch from a distance. *(Northampton Chronicle & Echo)*

113. Whatever is going on in Ashburnham Road on the night of Thursday 7 October 1965? A cow in calf was discovered running terrified along busy streets; it crossed the Wellingborough Road and careered along Park Avenue North. The frightened animal injured police constable Stan Major and scattered spectators before being cornered in a garage. The police constable, armed with a home-made lasso made from a car tow rope, finally managed to rope the animal in Ashburnham Road, and we see here two of his colleagues assisting to persuade the cow to come along quietly and enter an RSPCA cattle trailer. *(Northampton Chronicle & Echo)*

114. A large police presence was required on Saturday 28 April 1962 in the vicinity of Wood Hill and the war memorial near All Saints Church. Members of the Northampton Youth Campaign for Nuclear Disarmament had spent an all night vigil by the war memorial and then staged a sit down protest in Wood Hill. The police moved in and are seen carrying away some of the protesters including 'Wacky' Small and putting them into the awaiting Black Maria van. The Black Boy Hotel only stood for another 12 months before its demolition. *(Northampton Chronicle & Echo)*

115. A scene all too familiar at football grounds and the attendance of the police is required. On Saturday 29 January 1966 at the County Ground, Constable Fairey and his colleague evict a troublemaker while home fans clamber back into the crowd. The Cobblers are playing against Everton in a First Division clash and over 16,000 spectators are watching the game.

Alas, the visiting team won 2 – 0 and the home fans went away very unhappy. Worse was to follow at the next game when the Cobblers went to play Manchester United at Old Trafford and lost 6 – 2.

(Northampton Chronicle & Echo)

116. It's one thing controlling rowdy supporters, but its another controlling ecstatic ones. Here are two pictures showing how jubilant scenes at the County ground have caused the Northampton Borough Police to be put under pressure in attempting to protect the football players after the game. This picture shows a solitary policeman amongst hundreds of fans following the final whistle at the Cobbler's last game of the season on Friday 24 May 1963. The 3 – 0 win over Hull meant that the Cobblers remained unbeaten at home and were champions of Division III. Their centre forward, Frank Large, is hoisted on to the shoulders of the supporters despite the Police's efforts to keep space around the players and escort them off the pitch. However, all was well and the team later attended a Civic Reception at the Guildhall.

(Northampton Chronicle & Echo)

117. This photograph was taken on the evening of Saturday 24 April 1965, when the Cobblers drew 1–1 with Portsmouth in their last game of the season, and secured promotion to the First Division for the first time in their history. The police inspector had organised a cordon of constables near the players' tunnel so that the players could leave the pitch as safely as possible. No doubt the pressure of the jostling crowd tested the police resistance, but all the supporters look happy as they cheer their idols. Later, once safely up in the stands, the players threw their shirts into the crowd as the cheering continued. It is interesting to note that many of the fans have 'rattles', once a basic requirement for football fans but now regarded as 'dangerous weapons' and consequently banned from grounds.

(Northampton Chronicle & Echo)

GROWING UP

118. Photographs of performing artistes fascinate a little girl who gazes at them in amazement outside the New Theatre in Abington Street on Friday 13 June 1958. With only two months left for the New Theatre before closure, a larger variety of shows than was the usual was being advertised to boost final audience figures. The theatre opened in 1912 and, although converted to a cinema in 1933 for a short while, held its last performance as a theatre on 16 August 1958. The girl's mother would probably have attended a number of performances at the New Theatre, but alas the girl will never be able to have the opportunity to do the same.

(Northampton Chronicle & Echo)

119. The long school holidays give some children an opportunity to build some unusual creations. Four boys known as 'The Balfour Road Gang' who were brothers from the Lyon and French families designed and built a hot air balloon at a cost of seven shillings using their own pocket money. It was made with eight sections of tissue paper taped together over a balsa wood base. The maiden flight from Stanhope Road on Friday 15 August 1969 was very successful, using a Primus stove to get the balloon aloft. However, on the Saturday, when another launch was made, the six foot balloon floated steadily upwards but then went out of control, going within inches of hitting a television aerial and a chimney pot before coming to earth in the grounds of Trinity School. In the picture, the boys can be seen with the houses in Stanhope Road in the background on Saturday 16 August, alongside an interesting straw structure which must have been their 'den'. One wonders if such activities had any influence on their future careers.

(*Northampton Chronicle & Echo*)

120. The very severe winter of 1947 will be well remembered by those who lived through it, particularly being so soon after the privations of war. In Northampton a staggering total of 53 inches of snow fell over the 57-day period from 12 January to 12 March. After one of the heavier falls of snow, a family can be seen clearing a way through the huge snowdrift at their home in Windmill Terrace, just off the Boughton Green Road, on 3 March 1947. Although snow brings many problems and disruptions to traffic, no doubt the children at the time will have really enjoyed themselves.

(Northampton Chronicle & Echo)

121. 'Stop me and buy one!' On the outskirts of Northampton, at the junction of the London Road and Hardingstone Lane, a smoking Eldorado ice cream seller serves a couple of happy girls in November 1936, even though it is not exactly the season, hence the shortage of customers. Not a vehicle is in sight on the main road south out of the town, while in the background houses are being built in Winchester Road. A horse and cart complete this particularly rural scene. The famous Queen Eleanor Cross is a little further down the road on the right hand side, out of view. The girls were probably enjoying a relaxing walk in the nearby countryside and are well wrapped up for November.

(W. J. S. Meredith)

122. (left) 'Young and old playing trains.' The sight of a steam train fascinates any young child, and, if there is also a chance to have a ride, the children will be there. What better way for the Northampton Society of Model Engineers to show off their fine locomotives than to exhibit and run them at local fêtes in the town. Here, Mr Ken Markie at the controls of the LMS tank engine, constructed by himself, gets ready to set off down the line with some rather apprehensive passengers at the St Matthew's Church Fête on Saturday 16 September 1967. A fellow member, Mr G. Steward, looks on.

(Northampton Chronicle & Echo)

123. (right) Ken Markie again at the controls on a previous occasion with a group of happy waving youngsters at the International Co-operative Day Fête which was held at Northampton Racecourse on Saturday 2 July 1966.

(Northampton Chronicle & Echo)

124. The seesaw at the Barrack Road end of the Northampton Racecourse on Wednesday 23 August 1961 plays host to a wonderful collection of children. The little girl on the far right seems a little apprehensive, no doubt waiting for her end of the seesaw to drop. One wonders how many of them still live in this area of the town. *(Northampton Chronicle & Echo)*

125. The dangers of children playing in the street are clearly seen in this specially posed photograph taken in Northampton on Tuesday 31 July 1962. Playing behind parked lorries is particularly dangerous and a campaign to bring this fact to the attention of lorry drivers was made during this period. Various photographs were taken around the town to illustrate the possible accidents that could occur. These children are of course from the generation before jeans, with shorts and the inevitable sticking plaster on the knee.

(Northampton Chronicle & Echo)

126. (left) With their new trek-cart fully loaded with camping equipment, the Eaglehurst College patrol set off on their way to the Scouts' camping ground at Overstone to take part in the Thornton Trophy which is awarded for general Scouting and camp craft. The competition, which lasts over a weekend, on this occasion on 17 and 18 June 1967, takes place annually and over 100 Scouts took part from 17 troops. *(Northampton Chronicle & Echo)*

127. (right) For many youngsters, being a Scout has been an enjoyable part of growing up. Scouting offers a tremendous variety of activities for the youngster and, like any organisation, fund-raising plays an important role. In this picture, photographed on Saturday 30 July 1966, Scouts from the 32nd Northampton (Eaglehurst College) troop have set up car washing facilities for the day for their fund-raising effort. They are obviously having fun and proceeds from the day helped towards the purchase of a much needed trek-cart for the troop.
(Northampton Chronicle & Echo)

128. The school holidays are under way and children flock to Abington Park to play. A group has gathered near Tank Hill to have a game of cricket with both girls and boys joining in with varying degrees of alertness, on Tuesday 31 July 1962. How fortunate Northampton children through the generations have been to have free access to such an amenity as this in their local park. *(Northampton Chronicle & Echo)*

129. Even a flooded running track at the British Timken sportsground doesn't seem to have dampened the spirits of these young athletes as they sprint to the finishing line. This is the Northamptonshire Association of Youth Clubs' Annual Sports Day on Saturday 27 May 1967, with many youth clubs from around the county supporting the event. The torrential rain early in the day almost forced cancellation of the event.

(Northampton Chronicle & Echo)

130. Following 'The Cobblers', the Northampton Town football team, has for many people in the town been part of their growing up from childhood to adulthood. All ages of people have followed the team over the years and the ones who remember the rapid rise from Division IV to Division I in the 1960s will always have happy memories and tales to tell. Here we see happy Cobblers fans on the platform at Castle station on Saturday 9 January 1965.

(Northampton Chronicle & Echo)

131. Here on the same day we see the fans on the train, travelling to London where the Cobblers were playing against Chelsea in the 3rd round of the FA Cup. A large number of Northampton supporters made the trip and were amongst the 44,335 crowd at Stamford Bridge. Alas, Chelsea won 4 – 1 on the day, but at the time they were a very powerful side. Even so, the Cobblers fans remained in good spirits throughout and were rewarded by seeing their team gain promotion to Division I at the end of the season.

(Northampton Chronicle & Echo)

132. With the Cobblers' season over and the summer in full swing, the main stand at the County Ground proves to be a popular location for a game of BINGO! In this scene photographed on Monday 23 May 1966, how interesting to see a contrast from the usual cheering football fans to the more sedate sound of numbers being called out. Judging by the coats that are being worn, it wasn't as warm as one would expect for the time of year.

(Northampton Chronicle & Echo)

133. A fine action picture taken at the Spion Kop end of the County Ground on Saturday 3 September 1960. The Cobblers were playing against Stockport County and had an easy 4 – 2 victory with Deakin and Wright scoring two goals each. Another good crowd has turned out to watch their team, and one wonders how many of them would be at Wembley Stadium some 37 years later to see a 'Cobblers' team play on the famous turf.

(Northampton Chronicle & Echo)

134. Northampton Vespa Club celebrated their second successful year with a splendid National Vespa Rally on Sunday 20 July 1958. Over 400 Vespa enthusiasts from all parts of the county converged on Northampton and assembled at Midsummer Meadow during the morning. Then, headed by the Mayor and Mayoress of Northampton, they rode to the Racecourse where they are seen arriving in the picture. At this stage, some 170 riders left the Racecourse on a 28 mile road trial cruise with their final destination being Billing Aquadrome. Meanwhile all other riders headed direct to the Aquadrome where various field events took place and over 1000 spectators watched the spectacle. *(Northampton Chronicle & Echo)*

135. It is Whit Monday 6 June 1960 and thousands of scooterists and spectators have arrived at Sywell from all over Britain to attend the National Scooters Association Rally. In fact, the rally had already started on Sunday with a national road event which finished at Franklin's Gardens. There were literally hundreds of motor-scooters on show and a full day of events had been prepared for the Monday to keep everybody entertained. In the picture, there is an event going on with very much an Austrian theme with both males and females dressed for the occasion.

(Northampton Chronicle & Echo)

136. All eyes are fixed on Frankie Vaughan as he sings at a dance at St Augustine's Hall, Northampton on Friday 26 October 1962. Since teatime he had been busy visiting other Boys' Clubs in Northamptonshire, and he had been to Corby, Kettering and Daventry before he reached Northampton. It was all part of an effort to stimulate interest in the Boys' Club movement, to which Frankie gave much of his time over many years. It was about 11 pm before he arrived at St Augustine's Hall but all his fans were delighted to see him. *(Northampton Chronicle & Echo)*

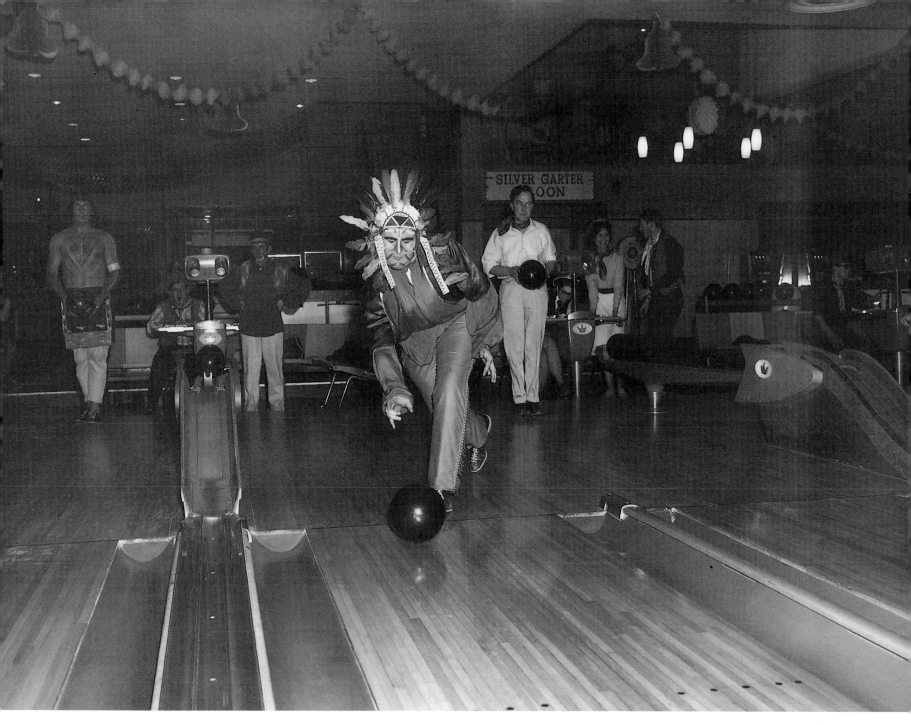

137. With New Year's Eve celebrations on Friday 31 December 1965 in full swing around the town, the Granada Bowl in Weedon Road was determined not to miss out. The management decided to hold a fancy dress celebration night with a 'Cowboys and Indians' theme. With the added handicap of a few celebratory drinks, bowling straight could well have become progressively difficult as the midnight hour approached.

(Northampton Chronicle & Echo)

138. Anglia Television visited Northampton on Thursday 31 August 1967 to record the 11th edition of their programme 'Carnival Time' which included a beauty contest and a set of zany games. On this occasion the event took place at Midsummer Meadow swimming pool, and entertainers Pete Murray and Bob Monkhouse conducted the fun and games. Winner of the Northampton final of the Miss Anglia competition was Miss Hazel Ward who receives congratulations from the two TV personalities. The 21-year-old Miss Northampton was one of nine finalists from the Northampton area who went forward to the final of the contest.

(Northampton Chronicle & Echo)

139. (left) Amongst the many attractions at a fair visiting the Northampton Racecourse during the week of 7-12 June 1965 was the 'Voodoo Girl'. Tyanga, a 19-year-old blonde girl from Western Australia performed with 'Simda', a 15 foot long python. It is not clear whether she is sizing up the snake for a coat, or perhaps it is sizing her up for supper.

(Northampton Chronicle & Echo)

140. (below) Here we see again Rochelle Lofting, who at the time was Britain's answer to Jayne Mansfield, taking her first look at stock-car racing when visiting Brafield Stadium on Sunday 5 May 1957. She was appearing all the following week at the New Theatre in Northampton and made visits to several local places of interest. She later presented cups to the winners of the races. *(Northampton Chronicle & Echo)*

141. A delightful scene photographed on Saturday 21 September 1935 showing happy employees from the Northampton True-Form shoe factory enjoying their day out at Blackpool. Not only was a special train organised for the party, but a special headboard was prepared as seen on the front of the locomotive. The dress fashions of the period are unmistakable and no doubt a good time was had by all. In the 1930s, the footwear industry still employed the majority of men and women in Northampton. In fact, the town was still the world's biggest men's shoe-making centre, and these outings were a traditional way for employers to show their appreciation to their staff. In this picture, we have been able to identify Ada Burrows, Lil Eagle, May Shimmell, Beatrix Followell, Glad Baker and Ida Followell.

(Les Clarke)

142. A True-Form 'factory outing' by coach to Dunstable Downs put employees in a party mood. Here they can be seen enjoying a singsong with musical accompaniment before the journey home. From left to right can be seen Messrs George Lane (with accordion), Doughty, Shoot, George Orlebar, Frank Hickman and Wally Eels. *(Les Clarke)*

143. Men do like machines whether they are motorbikes, motor cars, steam locomotives or traction engines. In this picture, two traction engine enthusiasts, Tony Whitmill (left) and Tony Harris, take a break from polishing their engine 'Margaret', a 1909 Garrett, on Saturday 3 October 1981. The occasion is a steam traction rally at Moulton Lodge, Northampton.

(Northampton Chronicle & Echo)

144. Thanks to the efforts of two traction engine enthusiasts, this superbly atmospheric scene could be reproduced on Saturday 23 October 1966 at Brafield. Mr Care's splendid traction engine built by Fowler in 1904 and named 'Pride of Northamptonshire', together with Mr Wooding's threshing box built in 1920 (which sports a metal plate with the name 'The Ruston Thrasher'), can be seen being used to perform the threshing of the harvest.

The straw was to be used for thatching purposes and was cut long in the field then stacked and fed into the threshing box. Although a combine harvester could have been used more efficiently, how could that compare for an enthusiast with the enjoyment of doing the job in the good old traditional way!

(Northampton Chronicle & Echo)

ROYAL CELEBRATIONS

145. The people of Northampton descended on the town centre to celebrate the Diamond Jubilee of Queen Victoria on Tuesday 22 June 1897, with the local businesses and shops putting on a wonderful display of decorations. Even though it was a beautiful summer's day, the people seem rather overdressed as they mill around at the top of Gold Street near the Grand Hotel. It was not the done thing to discard much clothing during the summer in these times, and this in particular was a day to be seen in your 'Sunday best'.

(Brenda Wise collection)

146. The Market Square was packed as were Mercers Row and Wood Hill with thousands of townsfolk intent on celebrating Queen Victoria's Diamond Jubilee, two of the spectators being rather precariously balanced on the shop fascia under the large flags. On 'The Old Duke of Clarence' public house, Vauxhall lamps surround the windows and an illuminated crown and V. R. stand on top of the fascia lights. Vauxhall lamps were like small tumblers in red, blue, green and amber which were illuminated either by candle or oil. Some of the fairy lights around the town however were illuminated by gas and a few of the larger establishments used electricity on their displays, a supply having been available in the town centre since 1891. *(Brenda Wise collection)*

147. Viewed from the cobbled street outside All Saints Church, people make their way around town without any fear of being knocked down apart from the occasional pony and trap, the horse trams and horse buses having been given the day off. Although it was a sunny day for the Diamond Jubilee celebrations, it has been rather windy in the Drapery, as the fluttering and furled flags testify. On the right are two styles of gas lamps, gas having been used to light the streets of the town centre since 1824.

(Brenda Wise collection)

148. Along with the thousands of individual Northamptonians, a number of organisations proudly paraded their banners in the Market Square for the singing of the National Anthem in a display of patriotism in appreciation of Queen Victoria's 60 years as reigning monarch. For such an occasion, people would feel obliged to wear a hat, and some have also utilised their umbrellas as sun shades in order to maintain their pale complexions. On the Market square, the Fountain is fitted with its second style of gas lamp while, in the foreground, 'The Old Duke of Clarence' public house on the corner of Mercers Row continued trading until 1912.

(Brenda Wise collection)

149. On Thursday 7 July 1927, the Prince of Wales (later King Edward VIII), paid a visit to Northampton. After laying a wreath on the Cenotaph at 1.50 p.m., the Prince of Wales stands outside the gate in readiness to inspect members of the British Legion in Mercers Row. The Cenotaph had been unveiled by General Lord Horne on 11 November 1926 on the eighth anniversary of the end of the First World War. Assembled on Wood Hill is a fine collection of automobiles from the period, while crowds of people throng the pavement on St Giles Square and George Row.

150. After all the celebrations and pageant connected with the visit of his Majesty King George V and Queen Mary to the town on Tuesday 23 September 1913, a large contingent from the Scouting movement make their way back to the St James area. The weather had been overcast with rain showers all day and the cobbles glisten wet, while some onlookers shelter under their umbrellas as the parade proceeds down Black Lion Hill and over West Bridge. Situated on the left is the entrance to Warner's Hotel, later to become Pickford's furniture depository, and the Postern Gate, a part of the old castle which was re-erected from its original position when the Castle remains were demolished. *(E. C. Lloyd collection)*

151. During World War II, King George VI and Queen Elizabeth made many unpublicised visits all over the country to encourage and congratulate workers in industry and the public services on their contributions to the war effort. On Thursday 4 March 1943, they visited Northamptonshire, including Kettering, Corby, Wellingborough and Northampton, and here we see them arriving at Castle Station. The King walks down Platform 6 in discussion with Station Master Hill, while the Queen chats to the Mayor, Alderman W. Lees, while Chief Constable John Williamson walks alongside. *(A. J. Bennett collection)*

152. Outside Castle Station, the King and Queen head for the waiting car to transport them on their tour. The visit was described as a 'working inspection' and it was the royal wish that the occasion should not be marked by 'pomp or panoply' or any civic and military pageantry which would normally be associated with such an occasion.

(A. J. Bennett collection)

153. The first place visited by the King and Queen on 4 March 1943 was the American troops' Red Cross 'Leave Centre' on the Market Square, where they chatted freely and informally to both American and British soldiers about their homes and other personal matters. On leaving, Queen Elizabeth was presented with a bouquet of violets and she is seen with the King heading for their next destination at J. Sears and Co. Ltd – the True-Form Boot Co. *(A. J. Bennett collection)*

154. After the visit to J. Sears & Co, the King and Queen headed for the Tanner Street works of the Northampton Gas Company, where they are seen in the works complex, the King talking to Mr George Slinn, an employee with 54 years' service, and the Queen in discussion with Colonel G. S. Eunson.

(A. J. Bennett collection)

155. On leaving the Gas Works during their visit on 4 March 1943, the King and Queen headed for the Town Hall for a half hour rest and to take tea prior to their departure from Castle station. On arrival at the Town Hall, their Majesties met the Mayoress and visited the Mayor's Parlour to sign the visitor's book. King George wore the uniform of a field marshal, while Queen Elizabeth's ensemble was of her favourite lavender blue and grey with a double row of pearls, and a diamond thistle brooch on the upturned brim of her hat.

(A. J. Bennett collection)

156. After attending the British and European Grand Prix at Silverstone on Saturday 13 May 1950, King George VI and Queen Elizabeth spent the night at Althorp House as guests of the Spencer family. On the Sunday evening, crowds have gathered at Althorp station to witness the King and Queen's departure as they are about to catch the Royal train and head for Balmoral. *(Northampton Chronicle & Echo)*

157. Many shops in Northampton decorated their frontages for the forthcoming coronation of Queen Elizabeth II on 2 June 1953. In this scene in the Drapery, shoppers do not seem to notice what is going on above their heads as workmen proceed with the display on the frontage of the original building of Adnitt Brothers. At the long established firm in the town, the upper floors were used for tailoring, dressmaking and millinery purposes, producing and altering garments for the shop below.

(Northampton Chronicle & Echo)

158. As part of the celebrations for the Coronation of Queen Elizabeth II, a divine service was held on the Market Square at 10.00 a.m. on 2 June. The solemnity of the occasion is reflected on the faces of the Northampton people in this section of the crowd who have come dressed appropriately for the prevailing weather conditions.

(Northampton Chronicle & Echo)

159/160. The divine service for the coronation of Queen Elizabeth II was attended by the Mayor and Mayoress with other civic dignitaries including a large contingent from the Northamptonshire Regiment and a smaller one from the Salvation Army. The shops around the Market Square were closed for the day and most workers were given time off to celebrate the occasion. James Bros. and J. Sainsbury, next to one another on the Market Square were popular town centre shops which followed different fortunes. James Bros. were renowned for their selection and service and have since ceased trading, whereas Sainsburys have evolved into the well-known chain of superstores, but, in their way, with much the same reputation as James Bros. enjoyed. *(both Northampton Chronicle & Echo)*

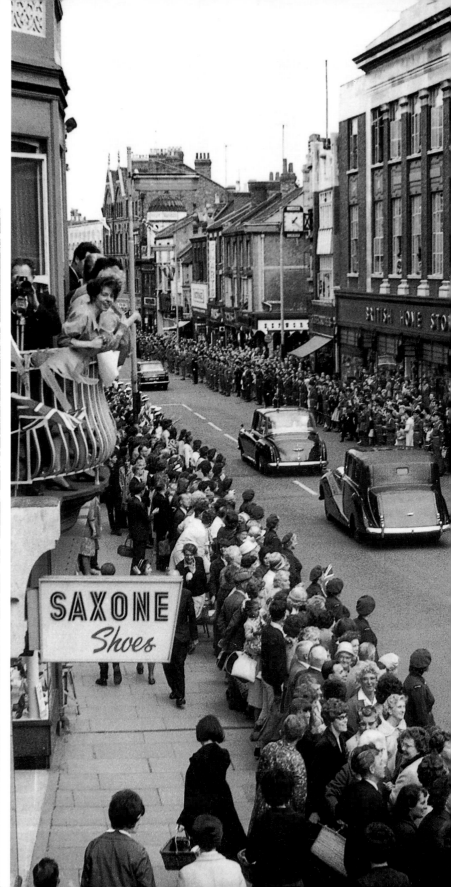

SAXONE
Shoes

161. (far left) Crowds of people line Abington Street hoping for a glimpse of Queen Elizabeth II who was due to arrive in the town with the Duke of Edinburgh on Friday 9 July 1965 following visits to Kettering, Higham Ferrers and Wellingborough. Many of the onlookers had been waiting nearly two hours before the first convoy of cars arrived, only to be disappointed as the first five cars carried officials who were travelling ahead of the royal motorcade.

162. (left) About ten minutes later at 1.20 p.m., the Royal motorcade with the Queen's Rolls Royce passed by to the delight of the gathered throng. Here we see the participation of the uniformed youth organisations, whose honour it was to line the route. The Queen and Duke were heading for the Town Hall and a welcome lunch appointment.

163. (above) During the long wait, boredom set in, leading to much frivolity amongst the staff at Sainsbury's and the adjacent premises.

(all Northampton Chronicle & Echo)

164 & 166. (right and next page) After lunching at the Town Hall on Friday 9 July 1965, the Queen and Duke visited Church's shoe factory in St James where a group of patriotic spectators wave their Union Jacks as the Queen and Duke arrive in their Rolls Royce. Following the visit, the Royal party travelled to Althorp to meet Earl Spencer before finally departing from the county later in the day.
(both Northampton Chronicle & Echo)

165. (left) As with all Royal visits, a good many youth organisations are involved besides members of the services and St John Ambulance, which necessitated a collection point to be set up on the Market Square for the visit on 9 July. At the collection point, a row of boilers have been lit to provide boiling water for the many drinks that would be required throughout the day.
(Northampton Chronicle & Echo)

167. On Tuesday 12 July 1983, a new 38 bed treatment unit was opened at St Andrew's hospital named 'Spencer House' and the occasion was attended by the Spencer family from Althorp. Listening intently to the opening speeches are Her Royal Highness the Princess of Wales, with her father and stepmother, the Earl and Countess Spencer.

(Northampton Chronicle & Echo)

168. During another visit to the town by Her Royal Highness The Princess of Wales, the *Chronicle and Echo* photographer has captured an unusual opportunist photograph during the opening of a new day care unit at Cynthia Spencer House in the grounds of Manfield Hospital on Friday 29 March 1985. Perfectly framed in a window of the new unit, the Princess of Wales, who 'looked stunning in a maroon and navy checked suit', chats to the Lord Lieutenant of Northamptonshire, John Lowther. *(Northampton Chronicle & Echo)*

FROM SKY AND ROOFTOP

169. An aerial view of Northampton town centre photographed in September 1963 showing many landmarks that were to disappear in the forthcoming years. Derngate, from the bottom right hand corner, leads up to the Guildhall, and Derngate bus station is clearly visible. In the centre of the picture, the stalls are up for a market day, and the Emporium Arcade and old Chronicle and Echo buildings are visible, but the Fountain has already gone. Newland leads away from the market to the top right corner of the picture, and all the old streets, to be lost in the Grosvenor Centre redevelopment, are still there. Opposite All Saints Church is the curved-front Boots building leading into Gold Street, at the end of which Marefair is still untouched; above here, the town's first multi-storey flats are visible.

(Northampton Borough Council)

170. A stunning aerial view of the centre of Northampton photographed at the beginning of June 1974. A radical change to the landscape is well advanced with little of the old centre of town remaining. The tall building in the centre left is Northampton House, and next to it the Grosvenor Centre can be seen under construction. Work on the new bus station, which from this view stands in front of the Centre, is just beginning. Further down Lady's Lane, the top deck of the Mayor Hold multi-storey car park is clearly visible next to the Saxon Inn hotel. Beyond the hotel is Barclaycard House in Marefair. In the foreground, the Mounts swimming baths, Fire Station and Police Station are in line along Upper Mounts, but the Horton & Arlidge building in front of them will soon be demolished. In the background, the new Carlsberg building can be seen at the top left of the picture.

(Northampton Development Corporation)

171. Claremont and Beaumont Courts, the two 12-storey blocks which tower above the central redevelopment area of the town, were completed in 1963. When this picture was photographed on Tuesday 29 December 1964, Mrs Eyre lived in one of the flats on the top floor with her husband and daughter. All the family enjoyed living high above the town and never found it boring. Apparently, at night the centre of the town was described as a fairyland aglow with thousands of lights. On a clear day one could see a great distance and there were splendid views. The only drawback at the time was the continual shunting of railway wagons in the nearby yard which continued both day and night and was a nuisance, unless of course you were a railway enthusiast! *(Northampton Chronicle & Echo)*

172. Also photographed from the top of Beaumont Court, this time in June 1965, it is interesting to note, compared to the foundations first being laid out in the previous picture, how the buildings in the foreground have shot up! By the quantity of coaches and wagons situated next to the goods shed at Castle station, the railway thrives. Meanwhile the chimney on the left at the West Bridge Destructor and Salvage Plant as well as Dover's chimney on the right both dominate the scene. *(Northampton Chronicle & Echo)*

173. An intriguing view from the top of Beaumont Court photographed in June 1965 shows a number of interesting parts of the town. Bearwood Street runs up through the middle of the picture towards Sheep Street and running parallel to this is Silver Street leading to the Fish Market. A large amount of timber is stored in the business on the corner of Scarletwell Street and St Andrew's Road, while Nicholson's Wool Merchants is the large building to the left of the Green Dragon public house. The Co-op building with the attractive black and white front, with the sign in the arch at the front 'Branch No. 11 Built 1919', was to survive only another six years, and the Mayor Hold to the right of the picture would also be re-developed.

(Northampton Chronicle & Echo)

174. Northampton Power Station and St Giles Church both dominate in this landscape view photographed from the top of the old Anglia Building Society building in Abington Street on Wednesday 8 July 1964.

Considering it is a working day, St Giles Terrace on the right-hand side looks particularly empty and quiet.   *(Northampton Chronicle & Echo)*

175. Roof timbers which have been in position above the New Theatre in Abington Street for almost 50 years are ripped out as the demolition gang is let loose with their pick-axes on Wednesday 13 January 1960. St Giles Church stands proud on the left, but the steaming cooling towers of the power station in the background would only last a few more years before modernisation would also mean their destruction.

(Northampton Chronicle & Echo)

176. The sad, sad sight of Northampton's New Theatre in the process of being demolished on Thursday 14th January 1960. Snow gently drifts down through a huge hole in the roof while a fire burns in the centre of what was once the stalls, now deep in rubble. In the circle and gallery above, seats have disappeared with timbers being ripped out to reveal a skeleton of girders. A sad end to a piece of Northampton's heritage.

(Northampton Chronicle & Echo)

177. A typical wet January day in 1960, and the photographer obtains a rooftop view looking south-west from the top of the Boots building in the town centre. Gold Street in the foreground shows the Grand Hotel on the right hand side and in the murky background a steam-hauled train heads south towards Hunsbury Hill tunnel. Buildings relating to the gasworks can also be seen on the left in the background with the various gasholders prominent. *(Northampton Chronicle & Echo)*

178. A member of the demolition gang balances precariously on one of the few remaining roof beams of the Peacock Hotel and surveys how much demolition has taken place. The gaping hole in the roof creates an unusual roof top view of Waterloo House and the top of All Saints Church, in this scene photographed in January 1960. Unfortunately, Waterloo House didn't escape the fashionable ravages of demolition and succumbed to the hammer of the demolition gang in 1964 causing yet another one of Northampton's historic buildings to disappear.

(Northampton Chronicle & Echo)

179. From the vantage point of the roof of the building on the corner of Abington Street and Lower Mounts, an excellent view across the rooftops looking east can be obtained. The scene, photographed on Wednesday 8 July 1964 shows the York Road/Abington Square junction, with the ABC Cinema prominent on the left. Wellingborough Road disappears into the distance on the left and most of the roofs are residential properties between the Billing Road and the Wellingborough Road. Although St Edmunds Church, seen in the top left corner, was to disappear, much of this view remains remarkably intact.

(Northampton Chronicle & Echo)

180. A stunning aerial view of the eastern side of the town centre and surrounding residential district photographed during September 1963. Cliftonville Road in the lower right corner leads up to the Billing Road which in turn heads towards the town centre. Northampton General Hospital is passed on the left before the road leads into Spencer Parade and St Giles Street. St Giles Church is visible surrounded by trees and just a short distance away is the prominent building of the Notre Dame High School in Abington Street. Upper and Lower Mounts in the middle distance leading towards Regent Square are clearly identifiable. The Northampton Racecourse is situated at the top right corner and the newly constructed multi-storey flats are in the top left corner. Along with the Northampton Corporation waterworks pumping station and reservoir, nearly all the allotment area in the lower left section is now taken up by the General Hospital and its car parks. *(Northampton Borough Council)*

181. Northampton's two new multi-storey flats are taking shape and this view from Beaumont Court on Friday 17 August 1962 shows that work has also started on the foundations of houses in Herbert Street. Over the street, the terraced houses are doomed, although one of them still seems to be lived in. Traffic is busy in St Andrew's Street which leads to St Andrew's Church, dominating the left side of the picture. Alas the church, together with the other housing in the foreground, was not sacrosanct to the developers and was to be replaced in years to come.

(Northampton Chronicle & Echo)

182. An excellent view of St Peter's Way roundabout, separating the large gas works complex in the centre of the picture from the town centre and residential area in this part of Northampton. At the time this picture was photographed on Tuesday 6 July 1965 the railway still dominated the area from the station to Far Cotton. One of the railway lines heads from the station on the right, past the carriage shed, and towards the locomotive shed where a haze of smoke can be seen rising into the sky. The other line heads past Briar Hill towards Hunsbury Hill tunnel. The terraced housing in Far Cotton dominates the area above the gas works and the Towcester Road can be seen heading off out of town. *(Northampton Chronicle & Echo)*

183. An aerial view over the Far Cotton district of Northampton pictured on Friday 22 July 1966. Three streets of terraced housing are clearly visible and on close observation very few cars are parked. Southampton Road, Euston Road and St Leonard's Road are the names of the roads from left to right. Northampton's first railway station, Bridge Street, stands in the right hand corner and the picture shows how the railway dominated this area of the town with sidings and wagons in abundance.

(Northampton Chronicle & Echo)

184. Two familiar Northampton landmarks photographed on Friday 22 July 1966 will long be remembered by Northamptonians. With the weather being warm and sunny Midsummer Meadow swimming pool is a popular venue and this aerial view shows how close to the town centre the pool was built. Across the winding River Nene the Northampton Power Station with its two huge cooling towers covers a large area, with a mound of stockpiled coal clearly visible. The Bedford Road on the right leads to Becket's Park at the top of the picture. *(Northampton Chronicle & Echo)*

185. A spectacular aerial view of the old hill fort at Hunsbury Hill photographed on Friday 22 July 1966. Over 2200 years ago during the Iron Age the hill fort was the centre of life and activity in the area and Northampton was just a wild, trackless forest sloping down to the marshes that fringed the river. Now the roles have reversed with Hunsbury Hill in this picture quiet and peaceful while down the hill Northampton exists populated with thousands of people. In the background, Towcester Road cuts across the picture with the cemetery surrounded by trees next to the caravan park. In the far distance houses run parallel to the London Road, and Mere Way can be seen joining the two main exit roads out of town. The expansion of the town southwards had not started yet and remarkably one was out in open countryside at the top of the Towcester Road.

(Northampton Chronicle & Echo)

186. High above the north-eastern outskirts of Northampton on Friday 22 July 1966 much development is underway. Boothville estate is in the bottom right corner of the picture with Booth Lane North running from west to east. Booth Lane School has been built leading off Booth Lane and is situated next to the new houses in Keswick Drive. The rest of the Lakeview estate is very much in the early stages of development. To the right, Kettering Road North is visible running diagonally towards Spinney Hill, with Manfield Hospital just about noticeable in the wooded area on the left of the picture. Spinney Hill Road sweeps towards the Parklands Estate at the top of the picture. *(Northampton Chronicle & Echo)*

187. Travelling out of the town along the Wellingborough Road, one passes Abington Park on the right hand side. On the corner of Roseholme Road and Wellingborough Road at the bottom of the picture stands the Abington Hotel with its distinctive gothic style of architecture. The County Ground dominates the scene with a cricket match in progress, and Phippsville and Kingsley Park districts are in the background. Park Avenue North runs northwards from Wellingborough Road towards the Kettering Road. In this scene pictured on Friday 22 July 1966, Manfield Shoe Factory is still very much in use and can be seen in the bottom left corner.

(Northampton Chronicle & Echo)

188. A final aerial view of a district of Northampton photographed on Friday 22 July 1966 shows the Northampton Racecourse with its pavilion quite prominent amongst the bowling greens. Kettering Road and East Park Parade runs north-south in the picture and the White Elephant public house can be seen at the corner of the park. St Matthew's Church can just be made out by the wing of the aeroplane in the top right corner, and in the bottom right corner is St Michael's Church.

(Northampton Chronicle & Echo)

By the Waterways

189. Not only was the big freeze-up in January 1963 a problem to the swans on the River Nene at South Bridge but 40 of them became oil contaminated on Thursday 31 January 1963. RSPCA officials carry out the painstaking task of netting each swan individually for transporting to Corby for cleaning, watched over by a few hardy individuals on the bridge. During the period of the freeze-up, over half a ton of bread had been tipped over South Bridge for the birds by a local baker.

(Northampton Chronicle & Echo)

190. There was no sign of St James Mill Road industrial estate in the vicinity of St James water mill in this wintry scene photographed on Saturday 16 January 1960. At this time the Victorian mill had been in the ownership of R. White and Lants since 1945. To the right of the mill stands the three storey mill house. *(Northampton Chronicle & Echo)*

191. (left) The River Nene passing through Becket's Park had been a favourite place for boating over the years even if the people are real amateurs as here, on Wednesday 3 August 1960, where the two boys are completely uncoordinated with their oar strokes and 'catching crabs' into the bargain. Rowing like that, it would take them some time to reach the boat house. *(Northampton Chronicle & Echo)*

192. (below) Here on the other hand, photographed on Wednesday 17 May 1961, during a warm spell just before Whitsun, the oarsmen appear far more professional both in the two dinghies and the canoe. *(Northampton Chronicle & Echo)*

193. (left) Another popular pastime by the waterways is fishing which whiles away many an hour, and here we see some children enjoying themselves in Becket's Park with their 'bandy nets' catching sticklebacks or tadpoles on Friday 22 May 1959.

(Northampton Chronicle & Echo)

194. Here things are being taken more seriously, going for the 'big ones' with rod and line, although they seem to have less to show for it than the children in the previous picture. This picture was taken at Midsummer Meadow opposite the power station on Monday 31 July 1961. *(Northampton Chronicle & Echo)*

195. The River Nene at Becket's Park was not the place to be in the middle of winter, as shown in this deserted and desolate scene in February 1954, with snow on the ground and the river completely frozen over. The lock is situated near the bridge which used to carry the Midland Railway tracks into St John's Street station, the bridge deck having been removed a few years previously. *(Northampton Chronicle & Echo)*

196. In contrast to the previous picture, all is hustle and bustle at the same lock on Thursday 10 May 1990 during 'National Environment Week' when Northampton Borough Council participated by having 40 tonnes of concrete slabs delivered by three narrow boats, thus reducing pollution of the atmosphere. The concrete slabs did however have to make the last leg of their journey by lorry to the council yard at West Bridge, which is rather ironic considering that the river passes right next to the depot, but was probably not navigable. In this scene the concrete slabs are being unloaded by crane from two of the boats on to waiting lorries. *(Northampton Chronicle & Echo)*

197. These two views show narrow boats 'Coleshill' and 'Cygnus' of Willow Wren Canal Transport Services Ltd operated by Mark and Doris Harrison, running the last regular commercial freight along the Northampton arm of the Grand Union Canal, and then via the River Nene to Whitworths' Victoria Mills in Wellingborough. 'Coleshill' the powered boat pulls 'Cygnus' the unpowered butty boat under the railway bridge at Duston West Junction and heads towards the railway bridge which carries the lines to Blisworth, from which point they will swing left with their loads of wheat, past the locomotive sheds, on Saturday 7 August 1965.

(Les Hanson)

198. Having arrived at the end of the Northampton arm of the Grand Union Canal, 'Coleshill' and 'Cygnus' have been tied up while their navigators have a well earned break. Later the boats will pass through Lock 17 and enter the River Nene travelling past the Crown Maltings building seen above the boats, on their way to Wellingborough. This traffic would continue until the end of March 1969. *(Les Hanson)*

199. British Waterways personnel arrived for work on Monday 17 October 1960, only to find that a maintenance boat had sprung a leak or filled with rainwater and sunk over the weekend on the Grand Union Canal near the south side of Blisworth tunnel. In the foggy conditions, British Waterways boat No. 126 'Archimedes' arrives and floating debris is retrieved prior to making an attempt to refloat the boat itself. At this time Archimedes was used as the 'length boat' for this stretch of water.

(Northampton Chronicle & Echo)

200. There cannot be many more spots on the Grand Union Canal as picturesque as where it passes through Brockhall Spinney, especially in the spring when the sun filters through the new bright green leaves of the trees on each of its banks. In this 1951 view, ex-Fellows Morton and Clayton boats 'Erica' and 'Fay' head south loaded with coal from the Coventry coalfields.

(Les Hanson)

201. Periodically, sections of the canal are drained for maintenance works, and here at Stoke Bruerne on Thursday 30 December 1982, a half mile stretch between the top lock at Stoke Bruerne to Blisworth tunnel has been drained, revealing the quite shallow depth of water held in the canal at Stoke Bruerne. The reason for draining was to carry out repairs to leaking walls and banks including a repair to the cellar wall in the Waterways Museum. During the draining procedure, pupils from Roade School helped to catch the fish for transporting to the undrained section.

(Northampton Chronicle & Echo)

Cancelled on the first passage through the re-opened Blisworth Tunnel.

CELEBRATING RE-OPENING BLISWORTH TUNNEL
BLISWORTH NORTHAMPTON 22 AUGUST 1984

Post Office, Blisworth, Northampton NN7 3BZ

Above. One of the postal covers carried through the tunnel.

202. To celebrate the re-opening of Blisworth tunnel on the Grand Union Canal, a special postal cover was issued to mark the occasion by the Blisworth sub-postmaster Mr Frank Bedford, who dressed up on the occasion in a postman's uniform from the 19th century and is seen here aboard the 'Spider', an external replica of a 19th century Blisworth tunnel tug. It is shown with its owner Mr Eric McDowell and family before proceeding through the tunnel with the postal covers on Wednesday 22 August 1984.

(Northampton Chronicle & Echo)

203. The tunnel on the Grand Union Canal at Blisworth had been closed since 1980 when it was declared unsafe for boats to pass through and this was followed by major structural repairs costing £4½ million. At the re-opening ceremony on 22 August 1984, the 'Spider' glides into the tunnel, leaving behind the warmth of the summer sun and the cheering crowds.

(Northampton Chronicle & Echo)

204. A large crowd turned up for the re-opening ceremony at the north end of Blisworth tunnel and, amid much cheering, the first two pleasure boats enter the tunnel to follow the 'Spider' through. The re-opening of this vital link in the canal network has saved many miles of detour for the users of the Grand Union Canal. *(Northampton Chronicle & Echo)*

205. Inside the Blisworth tunnel on the Grand Union Canal, repaired sections of brickwork show up against the remainder which is still blackened from the days of the steam tunnel tugs.

(Northampton Chronicle & Echo)

INDEX

206. In the bleak mid-winter on the Market Square on Thursday 4 March 1965. *(Northampton Chronicle & Echo)*